Macmillan / McGraw-Hill S

ELECTRICAL ENERGY

ACTIVITY LOG

MACMILLAN / McGRAW-HILL

SCIENCE TURNS MINDS ON™

MACMILLAN / McGRAW-HILL
School Publishing Company

New York • Columbus

PRINTED ON RECYCLED PAPER

MY NOTES

Illustration Credits: Joe Chicko, pp. 2, 27; Leslie Franz, pp. 6, 20, 21, 25, 34.

Photography Credits: Tim Fuller, pp. 1, 10, 15.

Macmillan/McGraw-Hill School Division
10 Union Square East
New York, New York 10003

Printed in the United States of America

ISBN 0-02-276160-8/4

8 9 POH 99 98

MY NOTES

CONTENTS

MY NOTES

Minds On! What happens when you turn on a flashlight, radio, or fan?•

How does this happen?

What kind of energy does the electrical energy change into in the flashlight? In the radio? In the fan?

AMAZING FACT

Electrical force travels through a substance at almost the speed of light. That's 300,000 kilometers (about 186,000 miles) per second!

MY NOTES

Minds On! Write about how you think electricity gets on clothes while they're in the dryer, or draw a picture to show how it happens.•

Where do you think the electricity comes from in the dryer? List your ideas here.

 Use with Student Edition page 13.

MY NOTES

EXPLORE **Activity!**

Sticky Cling

What To Do

Write down your observations and responses to the questions in the appropriate spaces.

Step 4

After peeling the strips off your desks, what happens when you hold the two strips close to each other?

Step 5

After your partner strokes both strips of tape with his or her fingers, what happens when you bring the strips close together?

Step 7

After you put both strips on top of each other onto the desk, pull them off and peel them apart. What do you predict will happen when you bring them close together again?

Step 8

Did your test match your prediction?

Step 9

Stroke the strips several times again and predict what will happen when you bring them close together.

Step 10

Did your test match your prediction?

MY NOTES

Explore continued

What Happened?

1. What happened when you brought the strips of tape near each other in step 4? In step 8?

2. What happened after your partner stroked the strips?

What Now?

1. Why do you think you got different results depending on what you did to the tape?

2. What other things have you seen that behave like the tape does? Tell below how what they did when they were rubbed together was like what the tape did when it was pulled apart.

Use with Student Edition pages 14–15.

MY NOTES

Minds On!

Draw a picture of your desk and a piece of tape. Put five positive (+) signs and five negative (-) signs on each.•

Imagine that you have pulled some of the electrons (-) off the desk and onto the tape. Erase 3 of the - signs on the desk and add them to the tape.

Does the tape have more positive or more negative signs?

Does the desk have more positive or negative signs?

AMAZING FACT

Ancient peoples of many cultures from all parts of the world believed that mythological beings, living in the sky or on high mountain tops, ruled the skies and kept order by hurling lightning bolts from the heavens.

Use with Student Edition page 17.

MY NOTES

Math Link

Write down your observations on how long the balloon stays up on the wall after rubbing it in your hair.

Does it stay?

What makes the balloon stick to the wall?

How long can you make the balloon stay up?

What makes the balloon stay up longer on the wall?

Now try rubbing the balloon for different amounts of time. Make your own table to record your data in the space below. Then make a bar graph of your results.

Rub the balloon again. Then have your partner rub all over the balloon with his or her hands. Does the balloon still stick to the wall? What changed?

Use with Student Edition page 19.

MY NOTES

TRY THIS Activity!

Clean Up!

Pretend you spilled papers and all you have to clean them up with is a balloon and a piece of wool cloth. Show how you would pick up the papers using static electricity to help you. Draw a picture of what happens. Try it.

In the space below explain why your method works and then share it with your classmates.

AMAZING FACT

Lightning helps change nitrogen in the air into chemicals called nitrates, which plants need to grow. When it rains, the nitrates dissolve in the rain and are carried to the ground, where they nourish the plants.

MY NOTES

Minds On! Work in groups to make a list of what it would be like if your town were without electricity for 24 hours.•

Why it would be fun . . .

Why it would be dangerous . . .

Why it would be inconvenient . . .

Use with Student Edition page 23.

MY NOTES

EXPLORE

Activity!

Path Making

Step 3

Draw each arrangement that you make with your wire and the flashlight bulb—even the ones that don't work. Then, be sure to mark the ones that do work.

Use with Student Edition page 24.

MY NOTES

Explore continued

What Happened?

1. How did you make the bulb light each time?

2. What happened when you used the masking tape side of your wire?

What Now?

1. What was the same about each of the ways you lit the bulb?

2. If you owned a flashlight and it did not light, what would you check to find out why it wasn't working?

MY NOTES

TRY THIS Activity!

Squeeze Circuit

How does the squeezing of hands act like the electrical energy in a circuit?

What happens to the energy when the circle is broken?

MY NOTES

TRY THIS Activity!

What Turns It On?

Make two lists—one of things that you think will make the bulb light and one of things that you think will not. Mark the items that work.

Things that worked	Things that didn't work

Can you use the items above that worked to make an easy way to turn the bulb on and off?

What happened when you tried to close the circuit with your finger?

AMAZING FACT

Electrical impulses travel very quickly through your body. When you stub your toe, your reflexes act quickly to pull your foot back before you even realize what's happening!

MY NOTES

Minds On! List some other ways in which wires are kept out of the way for safety.•

AMAZING FACT

Solid table salt does not conduct an electric current. But when you mix the salt in water, it makes water an even better conductor!

MY NOTES

Minds On! Draw how you think several lights are connected so they can all be turned on by the same switch. •

MY NOTES

EXPLORE **Activity!**

Different Paths

What To Do

Construct a circuit so that one D-cell can light two bulbs. Use the fewest number of wires you can. Draw your circuit diagram. Label it "Circuit 1."

Predict what will happen when you remove one of the bulbs. Test your prediction.

Construct a circuit containing one D-cell and two bulbs so that if one bulb is removed the other bulb remains lit. Use the fewest number of wires you can. Test your circuit by removing a bulb. Draw your circuit diagram. Label it "Circuit 2."

MY NOTES

Explore continued

What Happened?

1. What happened when you removed a light bulb in each circuit?

2. Which circuit had the two brightest bulbs?

What Now?

1. When you removed one bulb, why did the other bulb go out in one circuit but not in the other circuit?

2. Why were the bulbs brighter in one circuit than in the other circuit?

3. How can removing and replacing a bulb be like opening and closing a switch?

4. Which kind of circuit do you think works best to light your home? Why?

 Use with Student Edition pages 36–37.

MY NOTES

TRY THIS Activity!

Switch Better

Can you control one light in a parallel circuit? What would happen if you opened the switch in the circuit shown?

Describe how this is like the lights you use at home.

AMAZING FACT

Certain kinds of fish use electrical shocks to protect themselves. They can produce enough power to light several household lamps for an instant.

MY NOTES

Music/Art Link

Work in a group to design a picture with two or three areas you want to light up and then to build the circuit. Plan a circuit with switches, bulb holders, and D-cells to light the different places on your picture.

MY NOTES

TRY THIS Activity!

"Short" Stop

When you connect one end of the extra wire to the bulb holder and then briefly to the next bulb holder, what happens?

How is this like the parallel circuit with a closed switch and a bulb?

Now tell why you think this is called a short circuit.

AMAZING FACT

News Flash! On October 19, 1879, the Wizard of Menlo Park, Thomas Alva Edison, has tested a light bulb that lasted for more than 40 hours!

 Use with Student Edition page 42.

MY NOTES

Minds On! How could you go through an entire day moving things without touching them? How would you do it?•

Describe below some of the problems you'd have and how you'd solve them.

AMAZING FACT

Iron, nickel, cobalt and some of the rare Earth elements are magnetic.

MY NOTES

EXPLORE **Activity!**

The Pull and Push of Magnets

What To Do

Step 1

Record three combinations that work to pull or push a bar magnet across your desk with another bar magnet.

Step 3

Sketch a picture of the iron filings that you see around the magnet.

Step 4

Sketch what you see. Write down which two ends of the bar magnets were facing each other.

Step 5

Repeat step 4 with as many different pairs of ends as possible. Label which ends are facing each other in your sketches.

Step 6

On the back of this page repeat steps 3 and 4 for the horseshoe magnet.

MY NOTES

Explore continued

What Happened?

1. Which ends of the bar magnets pulled toward each other and where did the iron filings clump closest together?

2. What difference did you see between the pattern of iron filings with two of the same ends (S and S or N and N) near each other and the pattern with two opposite ends (N and S) near each other?

What Now?

1. Look at your sketches of the patterns the magnets made in the iron filings. How do you think the magnets pushed or pulled each other without touching?

2. Which parts of the magnets would be best for picking up paper clips?

MY NOTES

Minds On! How could you tell which bar of steel was a magnet if they weren't labeled and you could only use the two pieces of metal? What tests would you have to make?•

Describe each test below.

AMAZING FACT

Saturn, Jupiter, and Uranus have strong magnetic fields just as Earth does.

MY NOTES

TRY THIS

Activity!

What's Attracted?

What happens when you put salt on a piece of paper over a magnet?

Would sand act the same as the salt? How do you know? Try it.

AMAZING FACT

Animals such as sharks, rays, honey bees, homing pigeons, some migratory birds, tuna, and salmon are all able to detect Earth's magnetic field.

MY NOTES

TRY THIS

Activity!

Make a Temporary Magnet

Record how many of the paper clips your new magnet can pick up.

Test your magnet the next day. How much did the magnet "fade" overnight?

AMAZING FACT

Doctors can now use Magnetic Resonance Imaging (MRI) machines to "look" inside people to check for problems. The magnets used in these machines are so powerful that patients and visitors to places using them are carefully screened for metallic items.

 Use with Student Edition page 51.

MY NOTES

TRY THIS **Activity!**

What's the Point?

What happens to a bar magnet that's free to spin? In what directions do the poles point? Draw your classroom and show how the magnet points.

AMAZING FACT

One type of stove recently introduced uses magnetic induction to heat pots and pans, while the "burner" top remains perfectly cool. Only pots and pans made of iron can be used. Glass and ceramic utensils will not heat up on these stoves.

MY NOTES

Minds On! How would you use a big magnet that could be turned on and off? •

One kind of bacteria contains small chains of magnetite (lodestone) that enable them to line up with Earth's magnetic field.

MY NOTES

EXPLORE **Activity!**

Turning the Field On and Off

What To Do

What happens when you touch a nail to a pile of paper clips? Record your observations.

5. Count the number of paper clips you picked up and record that number in the chart below.

First Trial Observations	Number of Paper Clips Picked Up

6. Predict what you have to do to pick up more paper clips. Test your rule and put supporting data in the chart.

Changes Made	Number of Paper Clips Picked Up

MY NOTES

Explore Continued

What Happened?

1. What happened when you placed the nail in the paper clips when the circuit was closed?

2. What happened when the circuit was opened (when you took one end of the wire away from the D-cell)?

3. What did you change to make the nail pick up more paper clips?

What Now?

1. Why was the nail able to pick up the paper clips?

2. What could you do to pick up even more paper clips?

MY NOTES

TRY THIS **Activity!**

What Makes It Stick?

What happens when you try to pick up some paper clips with just the coil connected to a D-cell? How well does it work without the nail?

Without opening the plastic bag, see if the iron filings are attracted to the coil. Draw the patterns that you saw.

What does this tell you about what makes an electromagnet work well?

MY NOTES

TRY THIS Activity!

Writing on Tape

What do you hear on the tape after you run the nail near the tape? Describe what you hear.

What does this tell you about the tape?

AMAZING FACT

Nerve cells that produce electric current in your brain have also been found to produce magnetic fields a billion times weaker than the magnetic field of Earth.

MY NOTES

EXPLORE **Activity!**

What Makes Electric Current?

What To Do

Does your current detector work? Record your observations.

After doing Step 5, record your observations here.

Now predict what will happen if you insert the other pole of the magnet and test your prediction.

MY NOTES

Explore continued

What Happened?

1. What happened to the compass when current ran through the wire?

2. What happened when you pushed the magnet into the cardboard tube?

What Now?

1. What did the loops of wire around the compass needle form when a current flowed through them?

2. How is the compass needle's movement evidence of a current in the wire?

3. What produced a current in the wire when you used the magnet?

MY NOTES

TRY THIS

Activity!

Wet Current

Connect your metal strips to the current detector. Then put the strips into the vinegar one after the other. Describe how this is similar and how this is different from the result of the Explore Activity.

AMAZING FACT

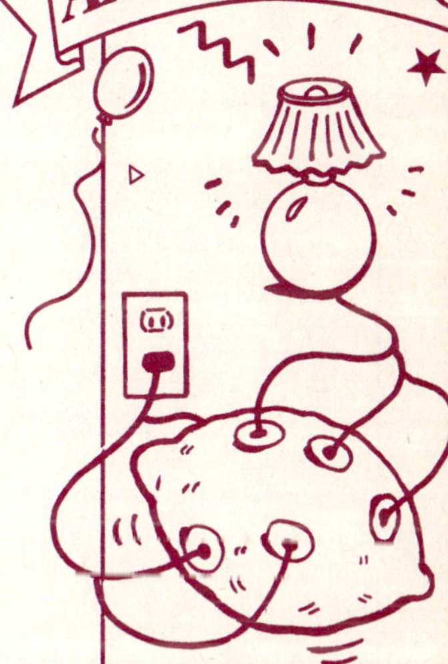

Many substances are good conductors. Even lemons can conduct an electric current!

Use with Student Edition page 70.

MY NOTES